About Skill Builders Vocabulary

by Jean Tappan

Welcome to RBP Books' Skill Builders series. Like our Summer Bridge Activities collection, the Skill Builders series is designed to make learning both fun and rewarding.

This workbook holds students' interest with the right mix of challenge, imagination, and instruction. The diverse assignments enhance vocabulary while giving students something fun to think about—from miners to manatees. As students complete the workbook, they will gain a larger working vocabulary and more appreciation of word usage.

A critical thinking section includes exercises to help develop higher-order thinking skills.

Learning is more effective when approached with an element of fun and enthusiasm—just as most children approach life. That's why the Skill Builders combine entertaining and academically sound exercises with eye-catching graphics and fun themes—to make reviewing basic skills at school or home fun and effective, for both you and your budding scholars.

Table of Contents

Draw a line from the circle by the word to the circle next to the matching definition.

Words	Definitions
danger ○	○ like, matching
raise ○	○ none
building ○	○ not old
young ○	○ brook, creek, river
stream ○	○ at risk
similar ○	○ people who ride
X ray ○	○ laughing African animal
canoe ○	○ region, specific location
receive ○	○ an enclosed structure
permit ○	○ lift up, elevate
zero ○	○ supply with, furnish
hyenas ○	○ picture of bones
understand ○	○ light, slender boat
scale ○	○ acquire, get
zone ○	○ to know
wealth ○	○ to allow something
provide ○	○ weighing device
history ○	○ an abundance of riches
success ○	○ victory, achievement
passengers ○	○ of the past

African Animals

There are many **exotic** animals in the world. For example, you can find **aardvarks**, **hyenas**, and toucans in Africa. The aardvark has a very long nose and tongue. An aardvark's tongue is very sticky, and he can use it to capture ants and **termites** he finds in old, rotten logs and hills. The ants and termites stick to his tongue and go right into his mouth.

Hyenas are **cowardly** animals that usually come out only at night. They make a very **shrill** sound that sounds like a laugh. Hyenas are meat eaters that travel in a pack that is led by a female. If the pack is large and it encounters a single lion, the pack will drive the lion from its kill to eat the meat. With **luck**, the lion won't get badly hurt, but it will miss dinner.

The **toucan** is a large bird with a huge bill and bright black, orange, and even blue feathers. Toucans have a distinctive call that you always hear in the background when you watch a jungle movie.

African Animals

Use the correct **boldface words** from the story to complete the sentences below.

1. A _____toucan_____ is a large African bird.

2. Aardvarks, hyenas, and toucans are _____ animals.

3. With _____ a lion will not get hurt in an encounter with a pack of hyenas.

4. An _____ has a very long nose and tongue.

5. Hyenas make a _____ sound that sounds like a laugh.

6. Aardvarks like to eat lots of yummy_____.

7. _____ are meat eaters that travel in packs.

8. Hyenas are considered _____ animals.

Wow! There are a lot of cool animals in Africa!

Camping

In good weather I get to go camping with my grandparents. We take a tent along to sleep in at night. We usually go to a state or national park, and Grandpa pays for a **permit** for our **campsite**. When we stop to buy our permit, the park ranger alerts us to any **dangers** that may be in the area. Sometimes bears come down from the hills to raid the trash cans, and people have to be **especially** careful to put their food away.

Often there is a speaker at the park who will tell the guests about the **history** of the area. If the park is near a lake or river, we can sometimes rent **canoes**.

When we get to our campsite, the first thing we do is **pitch** our tent and lay out our sleeping bags. It is always hard for me to go to sleep at night because I am so **excited**.

I love camping!

Camping

In the numbered sentences below, circle the word or words that mean the same as the **boldface word**.

1. It is fun to learn the **history** of an area you visit.

    name   notice   (story about the past)

2. The first thing we do to set up our campsite is **pitch** our tent.

    set up   throw away   take down

3. We like to ride in **canoes** on the lake.

    boats   rafts   skis

4. Bears can be a source of many **dangers**.

    events   hazards   stories

5. I am always very **excited** before going on a trip.

    sleepy   tired   eager

6. We like our **campsite** near the water.

    tent area   store area   game area

7. If you camp in a national park, you must buy a **permit**.

    sign   tent   permission

8. When crossing a street, be **especially** careful to look both ways.

    frequently   particularly   necessary

               Vocabulary Grade 3—RBP3454

Birthday

It is Jacob's birthday. Today he will be three. Every **member** of our family is going to be at his party. Our aunts and uncles have **further** to drive than anyone else, but they have promised Grandpa that they would not **speed** to get here faster.

Grandpa bought Jacob a new fishing **rod** and some **tackle**. Mother thought Jacob was too young, but Grandpa insisted that a boy is never too young to go fishing with his grandpa. Grandpa's fishing **pole** is old, but it is his **favorite**. He says it catches more fish than a new one would, and he plans to **prove** it on the first good fishing day.

Later in the day, after we finish playing games, we will all have cake and ice cream, and Jacob will open his presents. Then we will see if Jacob thinks he is too young to have a fishing pole.

8

Birthday

Find the **boldface words** from the story in the puzzle below. Words may go in any direction.

```
i d e e p s l s f l
f j f a v o r i t e
r o d g f x m e j r
r e t r l h l y b e
e v r q s k x h q h
b o h u c k p f r t
m r x a z m o q e r
e p t s s z l f t u
m e r k n w e h a f
p v p p l p t e l z
```

Baby Animals

How many baby **animal** names do you know? For example, you probably know that baby dogs are called pups, but did you know that another name for them is **whelps**?

In our barn we have a family of geese and ducks. Mother goose is tending her **goslings**, and mother duck is tending her ducklings.

Our **ewes** all have **young** lambs. Some of them even have two. The lambs are walking in the pasture, but their legs are very **wobbly**.

In March our donkey and our horse had **foals**. The donkey had a filly, which means the foal is female. The horse had a male, so he is called a **colt**.

This pig has piglets!

www.summerbridgeactivities.com

Baby Animals

Use the **boldface words** from the story to answer the puzzle below.

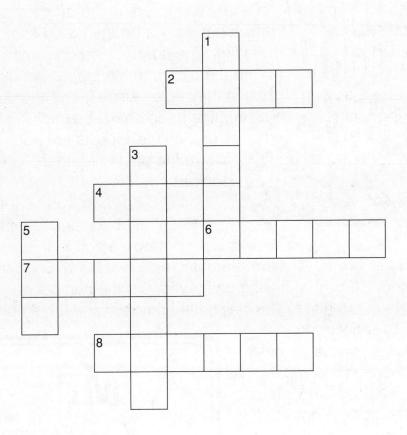

Across

2. newborn male horse
4. newborn horse
6. not old
7. puppy
8. A mammal is an _____.

Down

1. shaky
3. newly hatched goose
5. female sheep

© RBP Books
Vocabulary Grade 3—RBP3454

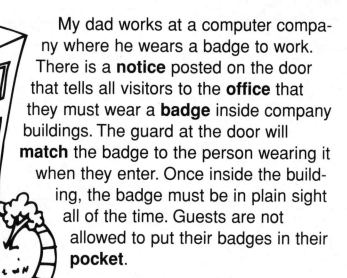

My dad works at a computer company where he wears a badge to work. There is a **notice** posted on the door that tells all visitors to the **office** that they must wear a **badge** inside company buildings. The guard at the door will **match** the badge to the person wearing it when they enter. Once inside the building, the badge must be in plain sight all of the time. Guests are not allowed to put their badges in their **pocket**.

Requiring badges for employees is a **common** practice. It is an **example** of increased security. Security officers tell us that having badges lowers the number of **thefts** at the office. This helps the company and the employees by reducing costs. When a company's costs are lower, the company has more money for benefits like extra days off.

Mr.
D. Orazzi

Badges

In the numbered sentences below, circle the word or words that mean the same as the **boldface word**.

1. If you **match** Mom's picture when she was seven to my sister's picture when she was seven, you can see how much they look alike.

   unite   (compare)   draw

2. My dad usually carries pens in his shirt **pocket**.

   a pouch in clothing   bag   sleeve

3. Strawberries are one **example** of fresh fruit.

   allow   problem   instance, specimen

4. It is **common** to see children wearing shorts in the summer.

   rare   typical   notorious

5. The police investigated the **theft** of my bicycle.

   stealing   hiding   ridding

6. Mom and Dad work in an **office**.

   warehouse   tent   building

7. There is a **notice** on the library door that says it is open from 10 a.m. to 6 p.m.

   sign   picture   sketch

8. Both police officers and firemen wear a **badge** to work.

   long tie   official identification   hat

Endangered Animals

Many people belong to organizations that protect animals that are in **danger** of extinction. Special laws **protect** animals that are on the **endangered** species list. For example, in certain areas of the southern United States, a water animal called a **manatee** is on the endangered species list. Because these animals are slow swimmers and usually stay in shallow water, boats have killed many of them. So few manatees are left that they are in danger of disappearing.

The organizations that **want** to protect the endangered animals have programs that let you **adopt** one of the animals. You get to select the type of animal you want to adopt, but you don't get to keep the animal. You do get a picture of your animal, and the money you **spend** to adopt the animal goes to help endangered animals in a **variety** of ways.

Endangered Animals

Write the letter of the correct definition in the space before the word.

1. __e__ danger   **a.** use money

2. _____ protect   **b.** take responsibility for

3. _____ endangered   **c.** different

4. _____ manatee   **d.** desire

5. _____ want   **e.** risk, a threat

6. _____ adopt   **f.** a water mammal

7. _____ spend   **g.** in danger of extinction

8. _____ variety   **h.** guard

Doctor's Visit

We are taking Savannah to the doctor's office today for her checkup. Our doctor's office is in the **front** of a large, red brick **building**.

When the **doctor** sees Savannah, he listens to her **heart** and uses a **ruler** to see how tall she is. Then he puts her on a **scale** to check her **weight**. Because she is healthy and doesn't have any broken bones, she will not need an X ray.

Last year I had to go to the doctor when I fell out of a tree, and I had to have an X ray of my arm because it hurt a lot. When the doctor looked at the **X ray**, he could see that my arm was broken, so he put a cast on it. All the kids at school signed my cast. That was the fun part.

Doctor's Visit

Each word below has a color. Use it to color the balloon that tells the meaning of the word.

1. front (red)

2. building (purple)

3. doctor (orange)

4. heart (blue)

5. ruler (gray)

6. scale (green)

7. weight (yellow)

8. X ray (brown)

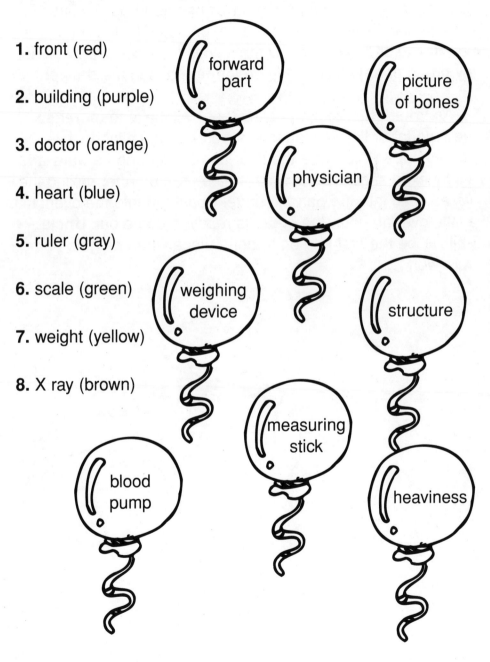

forward part

picture of bones

physician

weighing device

structure

blood pump

measuring stick

heaviness

Vocabulary Grade 3—RBP3454

Banana Nut Bread

There are two very **ripe** bananas in the kitchen. **Although** they are a little too ripe to eat out of the peel, they are just right for making banana nut bread. I use good-quality flour, but I don't care what **brand** it is as long as it is flour for bread. The cupboard has all the spices I will need, as well as my bread pan. The spoon I use for mixing is in the **drawer**.

As I **read** the recipe, I notice that I will have to **increase** the amount of flour because we live at a high altitude. I will need a cup to **measure** the flour and sugar, and I always add a little extra sugar so the bread will be sweet. After mixing the ingredients, into the pan the batter goes and into the oven. In a little over an hour, the bread is ready to come out. **Uncle** Phil will be the first person to get a piece when he gets home from work.

Banana Nut Bread

Find the **boldface words** from the story in the puzzle below. Words may go in any direction.

```
s  s  e  r  u  s  a  e  m  a
c  u  x  e  t  n  b  v  e  l
r  p  h  u  f  e  c  i  s  s
e  o  g  e  q  s  s  l  f  b
w  d  u  b  f  a  m  w  e  e
a  w  o  f  d  e  d  e  n  s
r  y  h  k  n  r  w  p  c  r
d  h  t  b  a  c  s  i  v  e
e  e  l  j  r  n  t  r  d  a
d  g  a  z  b  i  z  f  i  d
```

© RBP Books   Vocabulary Grade 3—RBP3454

Spring Garden

After the long winter, we are anxious for warm weather so we can begin planting our spring garden. We sit at the kitchen table with Mom and plan the flowers and vegetables we want. We plant a **combination** of seeds, bulbs, and seedlings. Large seeds like corn, beans, and peas we moisten with water, wrap in a cloth, and store in a dark place to wait for them to **sprout**. Allowing the seeds to sprout before we plant them will shorten the time that it takes for them to grow.

At the **nursery**, we buy herb and spice seedlings in two-inch pots. We also buy fertilizer for the flowers, vegetables, trees, and our lawn. Fertilizer will provide extra **nutrients** for our plants.

We check the weather carefully. We must wait until all danger of **frost** is past and the soil is warm enough to **germinate** the seeds. If the weather turns cold, the frost will kill our new plants.

Everyone in the family is **eager** to get the plants growing so the flowers and vegetables will bloom. The **blooming flowers** will decorate our house, and the vegetables will provide delicious food for our dinner.

Spring Garden

Write the **boldface word** or **words** from the story that best answer the questions below.

1. What will decorate our house? **blooming flowers**

2. Seeds, bulbs, and seedlings make up a what? _____

3. What do moist seeds do if they are wrapped and placed in the dark?_____

4. What will kill new plants?_____

5. What does fertilizer provide to plants?_____

6. What will warm soil cause the seeds to do?_____

7. How does the family feel about getting the plants growing?

_____

8. Where can we buy herb and spice seedlings? _____

Extra!

Write a sentence naming three flowers in your garden. Write a second sentence telling which vegetables you would like to plant in your spring garden.

_____

_____

_____

Microscope

My brother Jim is doing **experiments** in his biology class. They are **investigating** cells in insects. Because the insects are so small, Jim is using a **microscope** to **enlarge** the parts of the insect so they can be seen. The microscope can **magnify** things by more than 100 times their actual size!

As Jim dissects these tiny **creatures**, he puts parts of the insects on a glass **slide** and then looks at them under the microscope so he can see a **clearer** picture. As he examines the slides one by one, he is supposed to draw a picture of each part he sees in his lab book. At the end of the quarter, he must have three complete insects drawn.

Science is fantastic!

Microscope

Write the letter of the correct definition in the space before the word.

1. __g__ experiments   **a.** instrument with magnifying glass

2. _____ investigating   **b.** enlarging

3. _____ magnifying   **c.** to make bigger

4. _____ microscope   **d.** more distinct, or easier to see

5. _____ enlarge   **e.** animals

6. _____ creatures   **f.** inquiring about

7. _____ slide   **g.** tests

8. _____ clearer   **h.** small, glass rectangle

    Vocabulary Grade 3—RBP3454

Miners

Miners were among the first people to use a **domesticated** donkey. In their search for gold and silver, miners traveled on narrow, steep trails that had many **twists**. Only a **donkey** or a **pony** was small enough to travel these trails carrying supplies. Since these animals carried burdens for their owners, they were called **beasts of burden**.

Even though the animals were small, they were able to carry large packs of tools and food. The miner walked the **trail** on foot and led his animal. If his trip were a **success**, the donkey would carry the gold or silver the miner found back to town. If he came to town with gold or silver, the other miners in the town would ask where he found it. Instead of telling them the real place, sometimes a miner would **lie** because no one wanted to share the gold or silver he found.

Miners

Each word below has a color. Use it to color the balloon that tells the meaning of the word.

1. domesticated (purple)

2. twists (brown)

3. donkey (yellow)

4. pony (blue)

5. beasts of burden (gray)

6. trail (red)

7. success (orange)

8. lie (green)

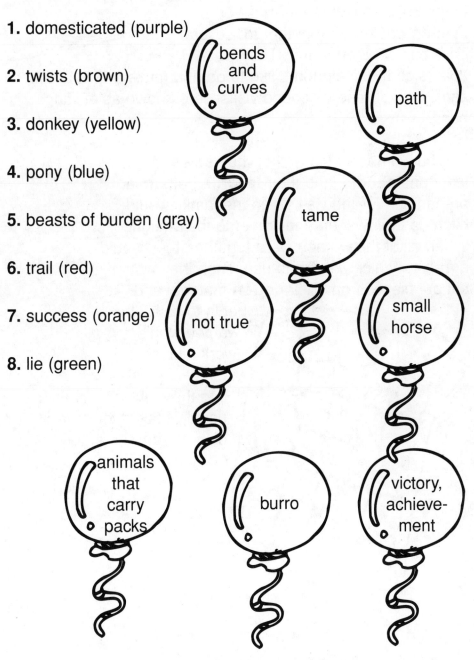

bends and curves

path

tame

not true

small horse

animals that carry packs

burro

victory, achievement

Quilting Bee

In the days of the pioneers, many women made quilts. Because a **quilt** took a long time to make, often women from several families would visit together for several days and work on a quilt. They were able to chat as neighbors like to do and make a quilt at the same time. These extended visits were known as quilting bees.

The women would gather their **scissors**, at least one **needle**, and their **favorite** pattern in preparation for the visit. Then the family would hitch up their wagon and **travel** to their neighbor's. When all of the women were together, they would **agree** on which pattern to use. Then they would cut out pieces from their **cotton** material and

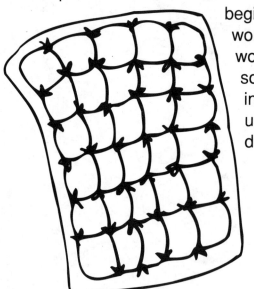

begin to sew. The women would work all day and sometimes late into the night. The guests usually stayed for several days to **finish** the quilt.

Quilting Bee

In the numbered sentences below, circle the word or words that mean the same as the **boldface word**.

1. We use **scissors** to cut out our pattern.

writing tool   (cutting tool)   measuring tool

2. I use a **needle** to mend a hole in my pocket.

sharp sewing tool   scissors   ruler

3. My sisters and I made Mother a **quilt** for Christmas.

curtains   dress   blanket

4. Cotton is a strong fabric that wears well.

material   pattern   needle

5. It takes a long time to **finish** a quilt.

complete   begin   agree

6. We will all have to **agree** to use the Lone Star pattern for our quilt.

begin   concur   quilt

7. The Double Wedding Ring is my **favorite** quilt pattern.

example   picture   first choice

8. I **travel** to school every day on a bus.

ride   walk   fly

Precious Stones

Today in our science class we learned about precious stones, such as diamonds, rubies, emeralds, and pearls. These precious stones are also known as **gems** and are **frequently** used to make jewelry because of their beauty.

A **diamond** is the hardest gem and is a clear, **crystalline** form of carbon. Our teacher explained that this means that diamonds are made from the same stuff that coal is made from. What changes the coal to diamonds is thousands of years of pressure forcing the coal into the form of crystals. This is what makes diamonds.

We learned that a pearl is a stone found inside an **oyster**. There are many pearl beds just off the **coast** of Japan. When the pearls are ready to **harvest**, pearl divers attach a net bag to their wrist. Then the divers jump into the sea and swim down to the oysters. They put the oysters in their net bags. Once the bag is full, the divers swim to the **surface** and put the oysters into their boat, then dive back down for more.

Precious Stones

Put an X in the blank before the word or words that mean the same as the **boldface words** in the sentences below.

1. A ruby is a **crystalline** form of a mineral.
   ___shiny and round **X** crystal-like ___square shaped

2. Boats float on the **surface** of the sea.
   ___waves   ___top   ___beach

3. An **oyster** is a type of animal that is found in the sea.
   ___shell fish   ___shark   ___seaweed

4. **Gems** are used to make beautiful jewelry.
   ___shiny stones ___colored stones___precious stones

5. A crystalline form of carbon is called a **diamond**.
   ___white glass   ___coal   ___precious stone

6. Divers **harvest** pearls from the sea.
   ___throw   ___collect   ___dump

7. Because Japan is an island, there is a **coast** on all sides.
   ___sea shore   ___cliffs   ___rocks

8. Waves **frequently** wash shells up on the beach.
   ___break   ___scrub   ___often

Vocabulary Grade 3—RBP3454

Our Yard

Every spring we work in our **yard**. We pull or **chop** down weeds to prepare the **ground** for planting our gardens. It takes us about a **month** to get each **garden** patch ready. After the ground is ready, we buy seeds. The back of the seed packages tell us when to plant. This depends on which **zone** we are in. We **determine** what zone we are in by finding our state on the back of the package. The packages show all the planting zones of all the states in our **nation**.

This year we have decided to use one patch for lilies, tulips and daffodils. Another patch will be full of corn and pumpkins, and a different patch will have three kinds of tomatoes, four kinds of peppers and two kinds of onions. We will have plenty of pretty flowers for the house and lots of fresh vegetables to eat.

Write the **boldface word** from the story that best fits in the sentence below.

1. Colorado is in planting _____ **zone** _____ three.

2. When weeds are tall, we _____ them down.

3. You can _____ the best time to plant by reading gardening books.

4. Many people have at least one small_____ patch where they grow things.

5. A _____ usually has thirty or thirty-one days.

6. There are seven different planting zones in our _____.

7. We have lots of lawn in addition to our garden patches in our _____.

8. The _____ must be prepared properly before you can plant a garden.

Patio Lunch

We are going to have our lunch today in the backyard. Our family really enjoys eating outside, so we do it as often as we can. My sister will get the patio dishes and some napkins from the cupboard and put them on the counter for Mom. Mom is going to make us each a **sandwich** with ham and **cheese**, and she is going to make herself a large, fresh garden salad. For dessert we **choose grapes** and lemon Jell-O.®

Mom asked me to go to the backyard and put the **umbrella** into the patio table and **lock** the gate to the fence that **surrounds** the yard. I will also help by putting the chairs around the table and wiping off the chairs and tabletop, which are dusty. This will make everything clean and ready for our lunch.

Our table and chairs are white, but our umbrella is a **zigzag** pattern of **primary colors**, red, yellow, and blue. When our friends visit, they tell us that the umbrella is very pretty.

Patio Lunch

Write a complete sentence with each of the words below.

**sandwich   cheese   choose   grapes   umbrella   lock
surrounds   zigzag   primary colors**

1. _____

2. _____

3. _____

4. _____

5. _____

6. _____

7. _____

8. _____

9. _____

Making a Salad

Mom and I are going to make a salad for our friends who are coming to lunch today. Many of our vegetables will come from the garden we planted in the spring. We have bright orange **carrots**, **onions**, dark green **chives**, sweet **peas**, **lettuce**, **tomatoes**, waxy **cucumbers**, and dark reddish-purple **beets** growing in our garden that are ripe and ready to pick.

In our refrigerator we also have some **celery** stalks and a large, white head of **cauliflower**. I will clean them and cut them into bite-sized pieces for the salad.

To make the dressing for the **salad,** I will mix the package of dressing with oil and **lemon** juice and shake it until it is mixed thoroughly.

Use the **boldface words** from the story to answer the puzzle below.

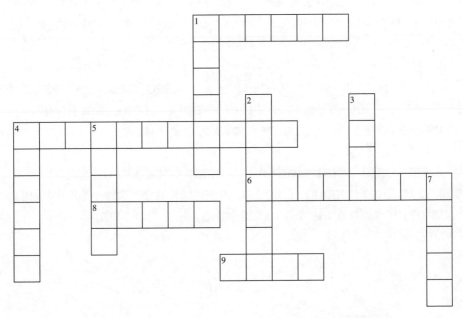

Across

1. long, slender stalks
4. white and fluffy; reminds you of clouds
6. bright red and juicy
8. I will make you cry.
9. small, green, and many are found in one pod

Down

1. Rabbits like this orange vegetable.
2. light green with lots of big leaves
3. large, dark reddish-purple, and round
4. tall, slender leaves; tastes like onion
5. Juice from this yellow fruit is sour.
7. all these vegetables mixed together

Rodeo

Many towns will have a rodeo for their Fourth of July celebration. Rodeos are an **exhibition** of skills that were **necessary** in pioneer days for cowboys who had to manage **bulls** and horses. Most of these skills are not needed today, but they are still practiced as a sport.

In one rodeo event riders use a lariat to **lasso calves** and tie their feet together. In another event a contestant rides a **bucking** horse. This is called **bronco busting**.

Last year I **competed** in the junior rodeo in an event called mutton busting. This is a special event for young kids. Kids get to ride sheep because they are too small to ride calves.

Rodeo

Put an X in the blank before the word or words that match the **boldface word** or **words** in the sentences below.

1. Dennis won the **bronco busting** event at the rodeo because he stayed on the horse longer than anyone else.

___bucking bull   ___bucking calf   __X__bucking horse

2. Cowboys have **competed** in rodeo events since pioneer days.

___played   ___been contestants   ___rode

3. If you ride a **bucking** horse, you may fall to the ground.

___jumping   ___swimming   ___running

4. Youngsters learning to be cowboys will use a rope to **lasso** a fence post.

___throw a rope around   ___ride a horse   ___ride a calf

5. Women frequently make quilts to put in an **exhibition** at the fair.

___covered wagon   ___display   ___home

6. Cowboys use a **lariat** to tie their horses to a fence post.

___belt   ___rope   ___saddle

7. Saddles are **necessary** for riding horses on a cattle drive.

___required   ___experienced   ___excited

8. In the spring, **calves** are branded by their owners.

___young sheep   ___young horses   ___young cows

Rabbit or Hare?

Both rabbits and hares are members of the rabbit family. This family of animals is **widespread,** and they are able to **survive** in forests, deserts, arctic regions, and even in suburban yards. Both rabbits and hares have four sharp, curved **incisors** in their upper jaws.

The **difference** between rabbits and hares is **confusing**. In most cases, rabbits are born blind and naked and have short legs when compared to hares. Hares are the long-legged, high-jumping animals that are most commonly seen in the form of a **jackrabbit**. Newborn hares have lots of fur and have their eyes open.

The snowshoe rabbit is really a hare that gives birth to two to six young born in the spring. It is called "snowshoe" because it has wide, furry paws that help it walk on ice and snow. In the winter its coat is all white.

Rabbit or Hare?

In the numbered sentences below, circle the word or words that mean the same as the **boldface word**.

1. Jackrabbits can run very fast.

rabbits   (hares)   pikas

2. Snowshoe rabbits **survive** in cold, arctic regions.

live   visit   run

3. When an animal has two names, it can be very **confusing**.

funny   puzzling   scary

4. In the winter, ice and snow are **widespread**.

too cold   everywhere   too wet

5. There is a lot of **difference** between forests and deserts.

not wet   not alike   not warm

6. Dylan lost an **incisor** last week.

shoe   hair   tooth

Extra!

Write a sentence and tell where you have seen a rabbit or hare. Was it a rabbit or a hare?

_____

_____

_____

Vocabulary Grade 3—RBP3454

Shopping

This **morning** I am going to the **grocery** store to do some shopping for the family. Michele would like a pint of whipping cream for her pie, and Dennis needs some **skim** milk and a **loaf** of bread. Mother has asked me to take a good look in the **vegetable** aisle and pick up some **lettuce** and any other fresh vegetables that look good. I plan on making a salad, so I want to get some fresh salad **greens** like lettuce or **cabbage**, radishes, green onions, and celery. As well as the vegetables, Mom has asked me to buy some frozen **dough** so we can have some fresh-baked bread for our Sunday dinner. We are expecting our aunt and uncle and our grandparents over on Sunday, and grandmother loves fresh-baked bread.

Grandmother has told us many times that every Sunday, her mother used to cook a roast and bake rolls. That was her favorite Sunday dinner.

Shopping

Write the **boldface word** from the story that best fits in the sentence below.

1. We bought one ____**loaf**____ of white bread at the store.

2. Corn is Uncle Phil's favorite _____.

3. If you get up early in the _____, you can watch birds eat.

4. Dawn made some _____ so we could bake some fresh bread for dinner.

5. Milk that has had the cream removed is called _____ milk.

6. If you want to buy food for the house, you go to the _____ store.

7. When Mom makes us a ham sandwich, she puts _____ on it, too.

8. To make a salad, you start with fresh salad _____.

© RBP Books   Vocabulary Grade 3—RBP3454

We live in the **mouth** of a small canyon, and a **stream** runs by our house. In the spring we **receive heavy** rains that fill the stream to the top of its banks. When the stream is full and swollen, I would **describe** it as a raging river. We divert some of the water into a pond. The pond will **provide** us with water for the entire summer. This allows us to grow gardens in many places on our property.

Just before the stream leaves our **property**, it splits into two branches. One **branch** journeys along the edge of the canyon for about a mile and then joins a bigger stream. The bigger stream journeys along for five miles and empties into a lake.

Streams

Use the **boldface words** from the story to answer the puzzle below.

Across

1. estate, land
2. entrance, opening
5. tell about, relate the characteristics of
7. acquire, get

Down

1. supply, furnish
3. a subdivision of, a part
4. massive, dense, in great quantity
6. creek, small river

Solar System

Earth is the **planet** we live on, but it is only one of the planets in our **solar system**. If you wanted to visit one of the other planets in our solar system, you would have to leave the **atmosphere** of Earth and travel into **outer space**.

Our solar system is a **collection** of nine planets and several moons that **revolve** around a star that we call our sun. Our solar system is part of the Milky Way **galaxy**. The Milky Way is **composed** of billions of stars, planets, and moons.

Jupiter is the largest planet in the solar system, and Saturn has rings. Mars is known as the red planet. The other five planets are Mercury, Venus, Uranus, Neptune, and Pluto. Pluto is so far away from the sun that it is frozen all the time.

www.summerbridgeactivities.com

Solar System

Write the **boldface word** or **words** from the story that fit best in the sentences below.

1. Nine planets ___**revolve**___ around our sun.

2. Billions of stars make up a _____.

3. Our sun is a star that is part of a _____ _____.

4. To visit other planets, a person would have to travel very long distances in _____ _____.

5. A _____ of planets and moons revolving around a star is a solar system.

6. A galaxy is _____ of billions of stars.

7. Venus is a _____ in our solar system.

8. When a traveler leaves Earth, he or she must travel through Earth's _____ to get into outer space.

© RBP Books   Vocabulary Grade 3—RBP3454

Learning to Sew

My Aunt Jean is an **excellent** seamstress, and she has agreed to teach me how to sew. Our first project will be an **easy** blouse. Before cutting the pattern out of our fabric, we used a tape measure to measure my **chest** and the length of my **sleeve**. We matched these measurements to the pattern to be sure the pattern was the right size. We then took a **tin** of **straight** pins and pinned the pattern to the fabric. I accidentally knocked the pins off the table onto the **carpet**. I had a lot of pins to pick up, but it was a simple job. I carefully cut the pattern out, cutting around each **notch**. I then removed the pattern from the fabric, pinned two pieces together and began to sew. Sometimes I had to ask questions, but with my aunt's help I was able to make the blouse in just one afternoon. Our next project will be a skirt to go with my blouse.

Write the **boldface word** or **words** from the story that best answer the questions below.

1. What do you call a nick or a gash in something?

notch
_____

2. If you draw a line with a ruler, what kind of line is it?

_____

3. What is the part of a blouse that covers your arm?

_____

4. What would you call something that is done very well?

_____

5. What do you call a task that doesn't take much effort?

_____

6. What can you store a bunch of sewing pins in?

_____

7. What is the name of the covering we have on floors?

_____

8. When you breathe, what part of your body moves?

_____

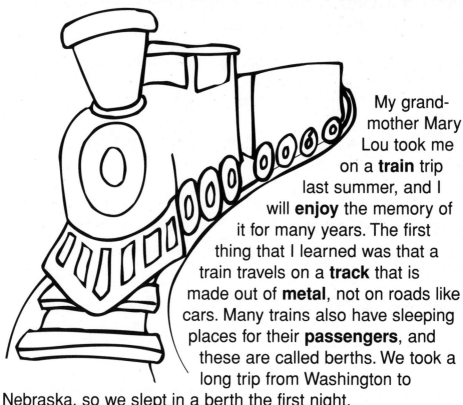

My grandmother Mary Lou took me on a **train** trip last summer, and I will **enjoy** the memory of it for many years. The first thing that I learned was that a train travels on a **track** that is made out of **metal**, not on roads like cars. Many trains also have sleeping places for their **passengers**, and these are called berths. We took a long trip from Washington to Nebraska, so we slept in a berth the first night.

Before breakfast we walked through several of the train's cars to **stretch** our legs. As we got close to the engine, we ran into the train's **engineer,** who was also stretching her legs. She told us many things about her train, especially about how powerful it was. She said we would be very glad that we had so much power once we began to climb the mountains. After visiting with the engineer, we went to the dining car and had breakfast. I ordered a big breakfast with orange juice and hot chocolate, but Grandmother only wanted a cup of **coffee**.

Train Trip

Write the letter of the correct definition in the space before the word.

1. __d__ passengers   **a.** a hot drink

2. _____ train   **b.** person who drives a train

3. _____ coffee   **c.** a substance extracted from ore

4. _____ enjoy   **d.** people who ride on a train

5. _____ engineer   **e.** rail

6. _____ track   **f.** extend

7. _____ stretch   **g.** a vehicle that travels on tracks

8. _____ metal   **h.** like

I love vocabulary this much!

Winter

In the winter, when the temperatures are **frigid**, many animals develop thick, furry coats. Rabbits, bears, and otters all do this. **Buffalo** coats **change** from thin and shiny to thick and shaggy. For most animals, winter is also not a time of **plenty**. Many animals, like the buffalo, become **lean**. Even bears, who are **asleep** for most of the winter in a cave, get lean during this time. It is a time when most animals have to search for long hours to find food. During very harsh winters, wild animals will frequently go to areas where people have built homes. They seem to **understand** that there will be food there. At these times even the **mighty** mountain lion is grateful for a handout.

Write the **boldface words** from the story that best answer the questions below.

1. What large animal has a thick, shaggy coat in the winter?

___**buffalo**___

2. If an animal knows a person will help him, he seems to what? _____

3. What do you call an animal that is strong and powerful?

_____

4. How do you describe a bear that has lost a lot of weight?

_____

5. When you take off sweaters and put on shorts, what do you do? _____

6. How do the bears spend the winter in their caves?

_____

7. What do you say about food when there is a lot to eat?

_____

8. How do you describe air that is very cold?

_____

The circus coming to town has created a lot of **interest**. A **crowd** will form as the circus workers begin to **raise** the big tents. The tents are large and colorful, and it is fun to watch. The workers are careful when they put up the tents so there will be **zero** accidents. The **weight** of even one of the tents is enough to crush anyone it might fall on.

My favorite part of the circus is the clown acts. The clowns have funny costumes and funny faces, and they pull lots of **jokes** on people. Everyone **laughs** when the clowns are around. Two of the clowns look **similar**, but one has a smiley face, and the other has a face with a frown. They drive around in a little yellow car and pretend to run over people. It is lots of fun because no one really gets hurt.

52

Use the **boldface words** from the story to answer the puzzle below.

Across

3. lift up
4. witty pranks
7. curiosity, fascination
8. chuckles, giggles

Down

1. heaviness
2. a large group of people
5. matching, like
6. none

Welcome to our play!

The drama teacher told us to come to the stage at 4:00 p.m. to **practice** our parts in the play. Every student in the play was **present**, but we were **silent**, waiting for the drama teacher to give us direction. We had **already** learned our lines, but we need-ed to practice work-ing together.

The play was a story about a man of **wealth** who was very stingy. Three ghosts were to **corner** the man on Christmas Eve and show him the evil of his ways. It was their job to teach him to be a better person. They were to teach him to be kind, loving, and generous. That was a big job to accomplish in just one night. After the ghosts left, the man would **remain** behind and put his whole **heart** into his new life. He would show his family and workers that he had changed and would now be a better man.

Find the **boldface words** from the story in the puzzle below. Words may go in any direction.

```
z  e  e  r  c  i  a  u  i  v
r  h  c  e  o  u  t  w  w  g
e  h  i  s  x  p  q  m  x  h
n  e  t  c  i  m  v  d  s  p
r  a  c  h  u  l  o  r  k  h
o  r  a  a  l  r  e  a  d  y
c  t  r  l  b  m  g  n  n  c
m  m  p  q  a  y  h  i  t  y
c  d  u  i  h  t  l  a  e  w
o  c  n  p  r  e  s  e  n  t
```

Word searches are my favorite!

Del and I are going to **design** a new house. We are going to base the design on a **famous** house that we visited, but we will make it smaller. We asked the owners of the famous **house** if we could use their design, and they did not **object**.

The **entire** house will be made of brick, and we are going to build it in the **valley**. The house will have a basement for storage, a swimming pool, a large garage for several cars and several large rooms for our hobbies. Del and I plan to supervise every **detail** of the house as it is built. By watching over it carefully, we will be sure that the house turns out **exactly** as we want it.

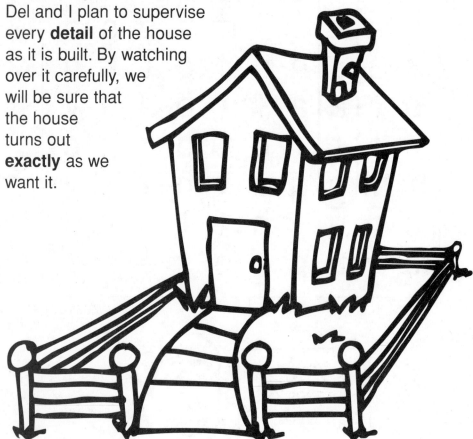

56

Write the **boldface words** from the story that best fit in the sentences below.

1. A _____ is an area of land between two mountains.

2. We ate the _____ pizza at dinner.

3. Mom cooked the roast _____ the way we liked it.

4. Every _____ of the house was just the way we wanted it.

5. I asked Mom to _____ a new dress for me for the prom.

6. Jim Bridger was a _____ mountain man.

7. Dad did not _____ to our playing in the garage.

8. Our _____ has four bedrooms and two playrooms.

Beaches

Choosing to visit a beach can be an excellent plan for a vacation. A beach can be a peaceful place to **hike** or a wonderful place to build a fire and cook a meal. You can walk along the water's edge and collect **shells** or other things that **float** in on the tide. In the **spring** and fall, the tides get very high and very low, and you can find many **interesting** things if you look along the beach at low tide.

Many people who **visit** the beach like to build a bonfire in the evenings to keep warm. They enjoy sitting by the fire and telling stories or singing songs. Sometimes they bake clams or roast hot dogs and marshmallows. A little sand gets into everything at the beach, like your blankets, shoes, and clothes. When it is time to leave, you just shake the sand out, or you can take a little of the **beach** home with you.

www.summerbridgeactivities.com

Write a complete sentence with each of the words below.

choosing   visit   beach   hike   shells
float   spring   interesting

1. _____

2. _____

3. _____

4. _____

5. _____

6. _____

7. _____

8. _____

Elks Creek Camp

I like to camp at Elks Creek. We set up our camp under some willow trees, right next to a creek. One of the willows has a hawk's **nest** in it. You can hear the hawk **cry** first thing in the morning and just before dark as the hawk flies near her nest.

Although our **camp** is no **hotel**, it seems **comfortable** enough to me. Who needs more than a sleeping bag, some cooking utensils, and trees blowing softly in the wind next to a singing creek?

One piece of camping gear that we always take is a gallon pail that **allows** us to dip water out of the creek for cooking and washing. Every once in a while I dip the pail a little too low into the creek and skin my **knuckles**. Each time I do that, I remind myself that I need to be more careful.

Find the **boldface words** from the story in the puzzle below. Words may go in any direction.

```
w  p  m  a  c  n  g  x  r  e  w
c  o  m  f  o  r  t  a  b  l  e
g  q  c  l  r  p  c  u  u  h  j
g  o  l  o  v (n  e  s  t) e  i
b  k  n  u  c  k  l  e  s  d  d
z  l  x  c  l  z  i  d  v  w  h
t  c  c  r  x  m  h  a  m  o  e
j  o  d  y  f  c  o  f  l  h  l
d  q  v  g  a  b  t  w  g  b  q
o  c  h  b  o  a  e  v  l  d. b
d  f  q  s  w  o  l  l  a  d  u
```

Halloween

During Halloween several students decided to play a **trick** on their principal. They bought a large lizard from a pet store and put it in the principal's car. It was really a **foolish** thing to do for **several** reasons. First, if the principal started driving his car, the lizard might startle him and cause an accident. Also, if the lizard were to get under the gas or brake pedal, the principal would not be able to drive properly, and that might also cause an accident.

Luckily, the principal found the **lizard** before he started driving, so there was no accident, but there was a lot of **anger**. The principal told the students that it was really a

crazy thing to do because people might have gotten hurt. To help the students think about their trick, the principal ending up **giving** them two weeks of hall sweeping. The only thing the students could use for sweeping was a small hand broom, so the **final** trick was on them.

Halloween

Use the **boldface words** from the story to answer the puzzle below.

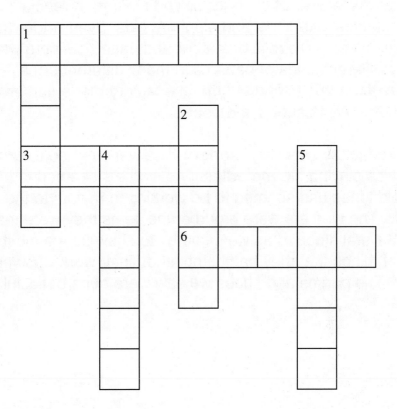

Across	Down
1. silly	**1.** last
3. bad feelings, fury	**2.** prank
6. unwise, foolish	**4.** providing
	5. reptile

Shoe Factory

My **sister** and I visited a shoe **factory** this weekend. There was a **wealth** of leather on every workbench and shelf. There was leather of every color and type, from regular cowhide to snake skins and elephant hide. Even **under** the workbenches were rolls of leather and patterns. There were many different kinds of patterns in many different sizes. It was a **surprise** to us to find out that the factory made purses and coats as well as shoes and boots.

The factory was very **modern**. The workers had a **radio** that was playing old **melodies**. The workers seemed to enjoy the old tunes and seemed to be working in rhythm to the music. The workers were proud of the items they were making. Several stopped as we came by to show us the most recent things that they had completed. Their work was very good. The purses and shoes we saw were quite beautiful.

Shoe Factory

Write the letter of the correct definition in the space before the word.

1. __e__ sister

2. _____ wealth

3. _____ factory

4. _____ under

5. _____ surprise

6. _____ modern

7. _____ radio

8. _____ melodies

a. astonish

b. music, songs

c. manufacturing plant

d. a device for receiving broadcast sounds

e. a female relative who shares the same parents

f. an abundance, a lot

g. below

h. up-to-date, new

Fishing

Dad and I are going fishing on Saturday. It will be our first time this year, and I am excited. The fact is, I can **hardly** wait. We have a special place. To get there, we go along a narrow path and over a ridge. Then we have to kneel down to go under a fence to get to our stream. Last year on a trip I hurt my **shin** on a rock, but I am going to be more careful this time.

The stream is quite **noisy** because it is running down a hill and over a lot of rocks. The water is clear, deep, and cold. But even so, we still have to **whisper** so the fish don't know we are there.

With our new fishing rods, we **expect** to **catch** a lot of fish. There are lots of trout in the stream, some as big as 18 inches, and we want to get our share. Dad said that I get to **carry** back all the fish we catch.

Fishing

Circle the word or words that mean the same as the **bold-face word** in the sentences below, .

1. My **shin** is very sore because I scraped it on a rock.

thigh   elbow   (leg below the knee)

2. We can **hardly** wait to go on our fishing trip.

barely   nearly   clearly

3. We **whisper** when we are near our fishing stream.

move softly   walk easy   talk quietly

4. We **expect** to catch a lot of fish on this trip.

count on   believe   require

5. Dad will **carry** the tackle box and fishing poles home from the creek.

bring   store   walk

6. If a lot of people go fishing at the same time, it gets **noisy**.

hot   busy   loud

7. I plan to **catch** more fish than Dad.

eat   hook   cheat

8. We have to **kneel** down to get under a fence on our way to the creek.

lay   sit   crouch

Collecting Stamps

My cousin Jacob is a **philatelist** and has been collecting stamps since he was three years old. He became interested in stamps because our grandmother gave each of us sheets of stamps for Christmas. We looked forward to seeing what new treasure we would get each year. It always **amazed** us that she was able to find such **neat** stamps. We thought that she **probably** had to search all year to find such a **variety**. Before she wrapped them for presents, she always **protected** them by placing them in a special plastic envelope. She told us that the envelope would protect the stamps and keep the glue from sticking to the page when we stored the stamps.

The stamps are very colorful, and many of them tell a story from our country's history. Some of them even show cartoon characters.

Sometimes we have to look at the stamps through a **magnifying** glass to see the small **details**.

Collecting Stamps

Write the letter of the correct definition in the space before the word.

1. __f__ philatelist   **a.** pretty, special

2. _____ amazed   **b.** making bigger

3. _____ neat   **c.** different items

4. _____ magnifying   **d.** surprised

5. _____ protected   **e.** likely

6. _____ variety   **f.** a person who collects stamps

7. _____ probably

8. _____ details   **g.** small parts

          h. kept safe

Our grandpa has a large, white barn with a weather vane on its roof. The weather vane is made of metal painted black and looks like a **rooster** standing on an **arrow**. It has been on top of Grandpa's barn for more than 40 years. Whenever there is a wind, it moves **freely** in the breeze and points the wind's direction. I am **amazed** that it hasn't fallen off or been blown off in all these years. Whoever made this vane **used** good metal and did a good job. That is why it has lasted so long.

Grandpa often **boasts** that his weather vane will even point the direction in the **middle** of a tornado. We don't want a tornado to hit the barn, but we are **sure** that if it does, our rooster will probably still be standing after the tornado is gone—so long as the barn is.

Weather Vane

Write the **boldface word** or **words** from the story that best answer the questions below.

1. What does a bow shoot? _____ **arrow** _____

2. What are you if you are very surprised?_____

3. What do you say about something that moves around without being stopped? _____

4. What do you call it when a person brags?

   _____

5. Where is something if it is in the center?

   _____

6. What is the past tense of <u>use</u>?_____

7. What do you say about something if you are certain it will happen?_____

8. What is a male chicken?_____

Matching

Draw a line from the circle by the word to the circle next to the matching definition.

Words	Definitions
mighty o	o to stay
protect o	o quiet
silent o	o to cut
remain o	o young cows
famous o	o extending far
pony o	o to make larger
finish o	o sharp, high-pitched sound
gems o	o powerful
chop o	o to complete something
calves o	o equipment for fishing
increase o	o whole
eager o	o a living creature
widespread o	o a small horse
tackle o	o to use money
animal o	o willing, excited
ewe o	o a female sheep
shrill o	o well known
spend o	o liked best
favorite o	o to keep from danger
entire o	o precious stones

Crossword

Across

4. the first part of the day

5. opening or entrance

6. an area suitable for camping

11. to go from one place to another

14. animals that are trained and useful to humans

15. one of the twelve divisions of a year

Down

1. unsteady, shaky

2. a jagged pattern

3. the seashore

7. travel faster than usual

8. a public show

9. liked best

10. hard to understand

12. vegetable with an orange root

13. unusual or different, rare or strange

Crossword

Across

2. a drink made from beans
6. to make bigger
7. land or buildings
10. slow-moving water animal
12. to rotate around
13. another word for <u>cold</u>

Down

1. another word for <u>thin</u>
2. part of the body between the neck and abdomen
3. to begin to grow
4. a muscular organ that pumps blood
5. a living being
8. mature fruit
9. a large group of stars and other celestial bodies
11. to understand written words

Matching

Draw a line from the circle by the word to the circle next to the matching definition.

Words	Definitions
change o	o opposite of <u>absent</u>
experiment o	o turn, bend
easy o	o blanket
straight o	o a baby dog or wolf
present o	o a controlled test
design o	o typical, not unusual
bull o	o timid and fearful
twist o	o to fasten shut
trail o	o hand-held cutting tool
quilt o	o not curved or bent
scissors o	o to desire
frequently o	o male cow
stretch o	o often
whelp o	o to make different
prove o	o extend or make longer
common o	o not difficult
cowardly o	o a marked path
lock o	o to establish the truth
want o	o to remain alive
survive o	o to plan

Vocabulary Grade 3—RBP3454

Answer Pages

Page 3 — Pretest

danger	at risk
raise	lift up, elevate
building	an enclosed structure
young	not old
stream	brook, creek, river
similar	like, matching
X ray	picture of bones
canoe	light, slender boat
receive	acquire, get
permit	to allow something
zero	none
hyenas	laughing African animal
understand	to know
scale	weighing device
zone	region, specific location
wealth	an abundance of, riches
provide	supply with, furnish
history	of the past
success	victory, achievement
passengers	people who ride

Pages 4–5 — African Animals

1. toucan
2. exotic
3. luck
4. aardvark
5. shrill
6. termites
7. Hyenas
8. cowardly

Pages 6–7 — Camping

1. story about the past
2. set up
3. boats
4. hazards
5. eager
6. tent area
7. permission
8. particularly

Pages 8–9 — Birthday

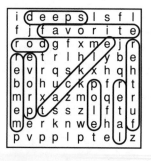

Pages 10–11 — Baby Animals

Across
2. colt
4. foal
6. young
7. whelp
8. animal

Down
1. wobbly
3. gosling
5. ewe

Pages 12–13 — Badges

1. compare
2. a pouch in clothing
3. instance, specimen
4. typical
5. stealing
6. building
7. sign
8. official identification

Pages 14–15 — Endangered Animals

1. e
2. h
3. g
4. f
5. d
6. b
7. a
8. c

Pages 16–17 — Doctor's Visit

forward part—red
structure—purple
physician—orange
blood pump—blue
measuring stick—gray
weighing device—green
heaviness—yellow
picture of bones—brown

Pages 18–19 — Banana Nut Bread

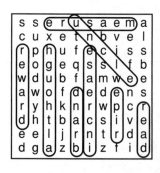

Answer Pages

Pages 20–21 **Spring Garden**
1. blooming flowers
2. combination
3. germinate/sprout
4. frost
5. nutrients
6. germinate/sprout
7. eager
8. nursery

Pages 22–23 **Microscope**
1. g
2. f
3. b
4. a
5. c
6. e
7. h
8. d

Pages 24–25 **Miners**
tame-purple
bends and curves-brown
burro-yellow
small horse-blue
animals that carry packs-gray
path-red
victory, achievement-orange
not true-green

Pages 26–27 **Quilting Bee**
1. cutting tool
2. sharp sewing tool
3. blanket
4. material
5. complete
6. concur
7. first choice
8. ride

Pages 28–29 **Precious Stones**
1. crystal-like
2. top
3. shell fish
4. precious stones
5. precious stone
6. collect
7. sea shore
8. often

Pages 30–31 **Our Yard**
1. zone
2. chop
3. determine
4. garden
5. month
6. nation
7. yard
8. ground

Pages 32–33 **Patio Lunch**
Answers will vary.

Pages 34–35 **Making a Salad**
Across **Down**
1. celery
4. cauliflower
6. tomatoes
8. onion
9. peas
1. carrot
2. lettuce
3. beet
4. chives
5. lemon
7. salad

Pages 36–37 **Rodeo**
1. bucking horse
2. been contestants
3. jumping
4. throw a rope around
5. display
6. rope
7. required
8. young cows

Pages 38–39 **Rabbit or Hare?**
1. hares
2. live
3. puzzling
4. everywhere
5. not alike
6. tooth

Pages 40–41 **Shopping**
1. loaf
2. vegetable
3. morning
4. dough
5. skim
6. grocery
7. lettuce
8. greens

Pages 42–43 **Streams**
Across **Down**
1. property
2. mouth
5. describe
7. receive
1. provide
3. branch
4. heavy
6. stream

Pages 44–45 **Solar System**
1. revolve
2. galaxy
3. solar system
4. outer space
5. collection
6. composed
7. planet
8. atmosphere

Pages 46–47 **Learning to Sew**
1. notch
2. straight
3. sleeve
4. excellent
5. easy
6. tin
7. carpet
8. chest

Pages 48–49 **Train Trip**
1. d
2. g
3. a
4. h
5. b
6. e
7. f
8. c

Pages 50–51 **Winter**
1. buffalo
2. understand
3. mighty
4. lean
5. change
6. asleep
7. plenty
8. frigid

Vocabulary Grade 3—RBP3454

Answer Pages

Pages 52–53 **Circus**

Across
3. raise
4. jokes
7. interest
8. laughs

Down
1. weight
2. crowd
5. similar
6. zero

Page 54–55 **School Play**

Pages 56–57 **New House**

1. valley
2. entire
3. exactly
4. detail

5. design
6. famous
7. object
8. house

Pages 58–59 **Beaches**

Answers will vary.

Pages 60–61 **Elks Creek Camp**

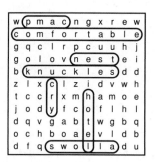

Pages 62–63 **Halloween**

Across
1. foolish
3. anger
6. crazy

Down
1. final
2. trick
4. giving
5. lizard

Pages 64–65 **Shoe Factory**

1. e
2. f
3. c
4. g

5. a
6. h
7. d
8. b

Pages 66–67 **Fishing**

1. leg below the knee
2. barely
3. talk quietly
4. count on

5. bring
6. loud
7. hook
8. crouch

Pages 68–69 **Collecting Stamps**

1. f
2. d
3. a
4. b

5. h
6. c
7. e
8. g

Pages 70–71 **Weather Vane**

1. arrow
2. amazed
3. freely
4. boasts

5. middle
6. used
7. sure
8. rooster

Answer Pages

Page 72 — Matching Definitions

Word	Definition
mighty	powerful
protect	to keep from danger
silent	quiet
remain	to stay
famous	well known
pony	a small horse
finish	to complete something
gems	precious stones
chop	to cut
calves	young cows
increase	to make larger
eager	willing, excited
widespread	extending far
tackle	equipment for fishing
animal	a living creature
ewe	a female sheep
shrill	sharp, high-pitched sound
spend	to use money
favorite	liked best
entire	whole

Page 73 — Crossword puzzle

Across
4. morning
5. mouth
6. campsite
11. travel
14. domesticated
15. month

Down
1. wobbly
2. zigzag
3. coast
7. speed
8. exhibition
9. favorite
10. confusing
12. carrot
13. exotic

Page 74 — Crossword puzzle

Across
2. coffee
6. enlarge
7. property
10. manatee
12. revolve
13. frigid

Down
1. lean
2. chest
3. sprout
4. heart
5. creature
8. ripe
9. galaxy
11. read

Page 75 — Matching Definitions

Word	Definition
change	to make different
experiment	a controlled test
easy	not difficult
straight	not curved or bent
present	opposite of absent
design	to plan
bull	male cow
twist	turn, bend
trail	a marked path
quilt	blanket
scissors	hand-held cutting tool
frequently	often
stretch	extend or make longer
whelp	a baby dog or wolf
prove	to establish the truth
common	typical, not unusual
cowardly	timid and fearful
lock	to fasten shut
want	to desire
survive	to remain alive

Vocabulary Grade 3—RBP3454

Notes

_____
_____
_____
_____
_____
_____
_____
_____
_____
_____
_____
_____
_____
_____
_____
_____
_____
_____
_____
_____
_____
_____
_____

Five things I'm thankful for:

1. _____
2. _____
3. _____
4. _____
5. _____